CHRISTMAS JOKES
HANDWRITING PRACTICE WORKBOOK
FOR KIDS
TRACE THE JOKE: JOKE#34
WRITE THE JOKE USING THE GUIDELINES TO HELP YOU!
I0764975

CHRISTMAS JOKES HANDWRITING PRACTICE WORKBOOK BELONGS TO:

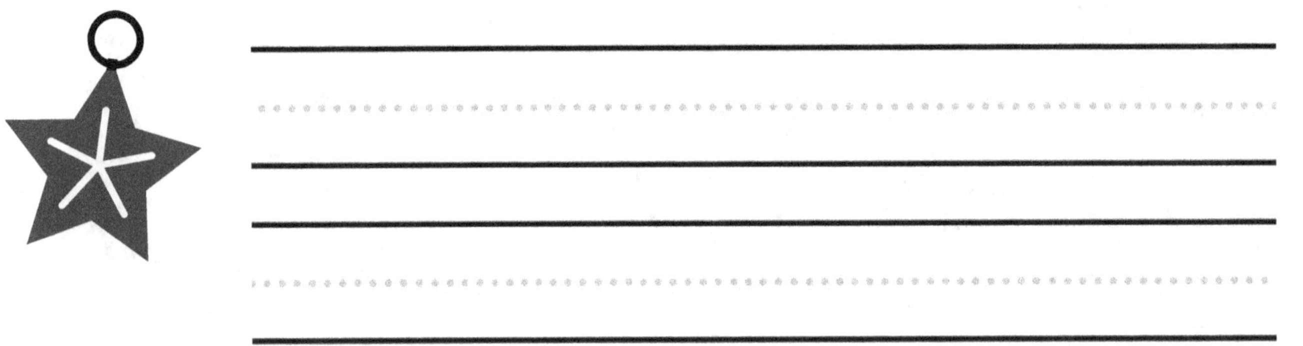

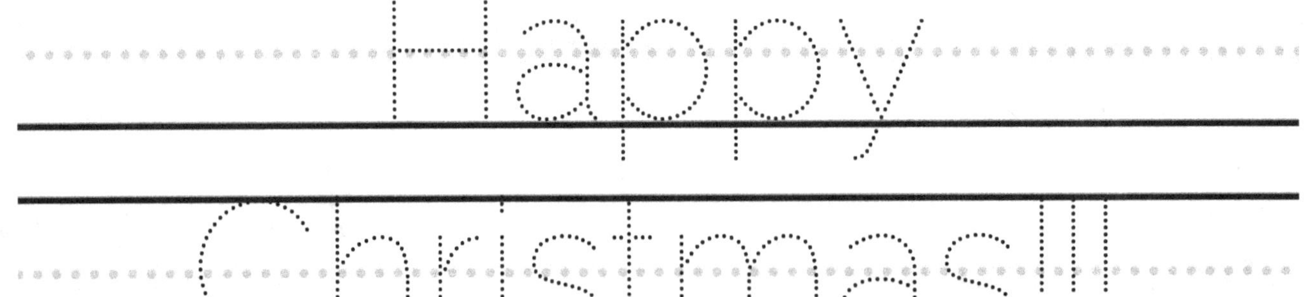

© **Sibley Carter Publishing**

TRACE THE LETTERS:

LETTERS

Aa Aa Bb Bb Cc
Cc Dd Dd Ee Ee
Ff Ff Gg Gg Hh Hh
Ii Ii Jj Jj Kk Kk Ll Ll
Mm Mm Nn Nn
Oo Oo Pp Pp Qq
Qq Rr Rr Ss Ss
Tt Tt Uu Uu Vv Vv
Ww Ww Xx Xx
Yy Yy Zz Zz

How does Rudolph
find out that
Christmas is coming?
He refers to his
calen-deer

WRITE THE JOKE USING THE GUIDELINES TO HELP YOU:

JOKE #2

What do you call
Santa who is on the
beach?
Sandy Claus

WRITE THE JOKE USING THE GUIDELINES TO HELP YOU:

JOKE #3

What is sung at a
snowman's birthday
party?
Freeze a jolly good
fellow

WRITE THE JOKE USING THE GUIDELINES TO HELP YOU:

JOKE#4

Why didn't the
skeleton go to the
Christmas party?
Because he had no
body to go with

WRITE THE JOKE USING THE GUIDELINES TO HELP YOU:

JOKE #5

How can you help
someone who has
lost the spirit of
Christmas?
Nurse them back to
the elf

WRITE THE JOKE USING THE GUIDELINES TO HELP YOU:

JOKE #6

Why does Santa Claus work at the North Pole? Because he was kicked out of the South Pole by penguins

WRITE THE JOKE USING THE GUIDELINES TO HELP YOU:

JOKE #7

How do the sheep
say "Merry
Christmas"?
Fleece Navidad

WRITE THE JOKE USING THE GUIDELINES TO HELP YOU:

JOKE #8

What kind of
a motorcycle does
Santa ride?
On a Holly Davidson

WRITE THE JOKE USING THE GUIDELINES TO HELP YOU:

JOKE #9

Why wouldn't the Christmas tree stand up?
Because it has no legs

WRITE THE JOKE USING THE GUIDELINES TO HELP YOU:

TRACE THE JOKE: # JOKE #10

Why do crabs never celebrate Christmas? Because they're shell-fish

WRITE THE JOKE USING THE GUIDELINES TO HELP YOU:

JOKE #11

What snack does
Santa like best?
Crisp Pringles

WRITE THE JOKE USING THE GUIDELINES TO HELP YOU:

What do snowmen
eat for dinner?
Icebergers

WRITE THE JOKE USING THE GUIDELINES TO HELP YOU:

What is the wettest animal in Santa's workshop? Rain-deer

WRITE THE JOKE USING THE GUIDELINES TO HELP YOU:

TRACE THE JOKE: # JOKE #14

Why was Santa's
little helper sad?
Because he had very
low elf esteem

WRITE THE JOKE USING THE GUIDELINES TO HELP YOU:

What does an elf
learn in school?
The elfabet

WRITE THE JOKE USING THE GUIDELINES TO HELP YOU:

JOKE #16

Why did Rudolph have a bad grade on his certificate? Because he went down in history

WRITE THE JOKE USING THE GUIDELINES TO HELP YOU:

JOKE #17

What do you get when you cross a Christmas tree with an iPad?

A pineapple

WRITE THE JOKE USING THE GUIDELINES TO HELP YOU:

What was the grumpy sheep's answer when her friends wished her a Merry Christmas? Baaaa humbug

WRITE THE JOKE USING THE GUIDELINES TO HELP YOU:

JOKE #19

What do you call a
snowman who has a
six-pack?
The abdominal
snowman

WRITE THE JOKE USING THE GUIDELINES TO HELP YOU:

TRACE THE JOKE: JOKE #20

What do you call a
reindeer that is blind?
I have no eye deer

WRITE THE JOKE USING THE GUIDELINES TO HELP YOU:

JOKE #21

What is a vampire's favorite song on New Year's Eve?
Auld Fang Syne

WRITE THE JOKE USING THE GUIDELINES TO HELP YOU:

JOKE #22

Where does Santa go
on vacation?
To a ho-ho-ho-tel

WRITE THE JOKE USING THE GUIDELINES TO HELP YOU:

 # JOKE #23

What do fish like to
sing most during the
holidays?
Christmas corals

WRITE THE JOKE USING THE GUIDELINES TO HELP YOU:

 JOKE #24

What sport do elves play?
North-pole vaulting

WRITE THE JOKE USING THE GUIDELINES TO HELP YOU:

JOKE #25

What candy does
the Christmas tree
like best?
Orna-mints

WRITE THE JOKE USING THE GUIDELINES TO HELP YOU:

What is a snowman's favorite breakfast dish?

Frosted Flakes

WRITE THE JOKE USING THE GUIDELINES TO HELP YOU:

In which year does
New Year's Day
come before
Christmas?
In EVERY year

WRITE THE JOKE USING THE GUIDELINES TO HELP YOU:

JOKE #28

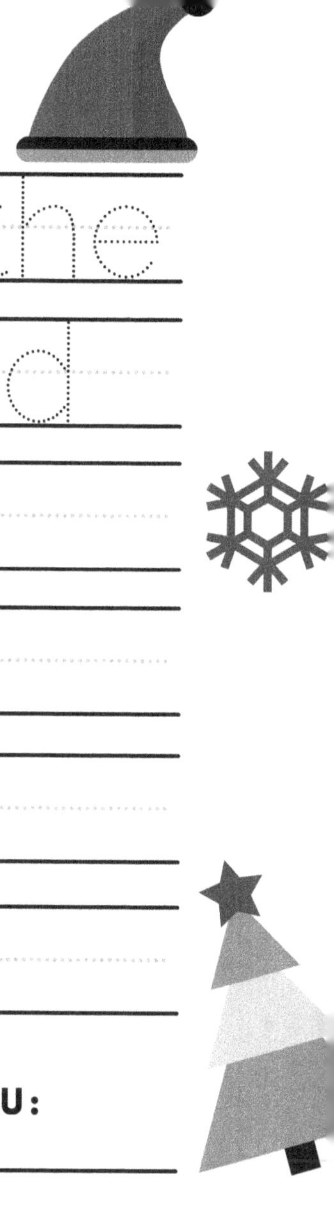

What do you call the
Santa who stopped
moving?
Santa Pause

WRITE THE JOKE USING THE GUIDELINES TO HELP YOU:

What do you call a snowman in June? A puddle

TRACE THE JOKE: JOKE #30

What does Jack
Frost like best in
school?
Snow and tell

WRITE THE JOKE USING THE GUIDELINES TO HELP YOU:

Why is it getting more difficult to buy Advent calendars? Because their days are numbered

WRITE THE JOKE USING THE GUIDELINES TO HELP YOU:

JOKE #32

What does a child
who is afraid of
Santa have?
He has a
Claus-trophobia

WRITE THE JOKE USING THE GUIDELINES TO HELP YOU:

What laundry detergent does Santa choose? Yule-Tide

WRITE THE JOKE USING THE GUIDELINES TO HELP YOU:

What happens when Santa gets stuck in the chimney? He gets Santa Claustrophobia

WRITE THE JOKE USING THE GUIDELINES TO HELP YOU:

JOKE #35

When does a
snowman lose
weight?
When it gets warmer

WRITE THE JOKE USING THE GUIDELINES TO HELP YOU:

JOKE #36

Where does a snowman keep all his money?
In a snowbank

WRITE THE JOKE USING THE GUIDELINES TO HELP YOU:

JOKE #37

Why can't Christmas
trees sew?
Because they always
drop their needles

WRITE THE JOKE USING THE GUIDELINES TO HELP YOU:

JOKE #38

Why does Scrooge like reindeer so much?
Because every single buck is dear to him

WRITE THE JOKE USING THE GUIDELINES TO HELP YOU:

How many presents can Santa fit in his sack for bad kids? Zero

WRITE THE JOKE USING THE GUIDELINES TO HELP YOU:

JOKE #40

What kind of music
do elves listen to?
Wrap music

WRITE THE JOKE USING THE GUIDELINES TO HELP YOU:

JOKE #41

What happens when
Santa becomes a
detective?
Santa CLUES

WRITE THE JOKE USING THE GUIDELINES TO HELP YOU:

Why can't you eat
Christmas
decorations?
Because you can get
tinselitus

WRITE THE JOKE USING THE GUIDELINES TO HELP YOU:

What do snowmen
do when the sun
gets too hot?
They take a chill pill

WRITE THE JOKE USING THE GUIDELINES TO HELP YOU:

TRACE THE JOKE: # JOKE #44

What do we get
when we cross
Santa with a duck?
A Christmas
Quacker

WRITE THE JOKE USING THE GUIDELINES TO HELP YOU:

What is the
monkey's favorite
Christmas song?
Jungle bells

WRITE THE JOKE USING THE GUIDELINES TO HELP YOU:

JOKE #46

What ball doesn't
bounce?
A snowball

WRITE THE JOKE USING THE GUIDELINES TO HELP YOU:

What are snowman's
favorite snacks?
Ice Krispy Treats

WRITE THE JOKE USING THE GUIDELINES TO HELP YOU:

What kind of vehicle
do Santa's elves
drive?
Minivan

WRITE THE JOKE USING THE GUIDELINES TO HELP YOU:

What do you call an
elf that is greedy?
Elfish

WRITE THE JOKE USING THE GUIDELINES TO HELP YOU:

Why do Christmas trees go to the barber?

To get trimmed

WRITE THE JOKE USING THE GUIDELINES TO HELP YOU:

I HOPE YOU ENJOYED THIS BOOK!

© Sibley Carter Publishing